Learn to Move!

I DO
KARATE!

T0204909

By Bray Jacobson

Gareth Stevens
PUBLISHING

Please visit our website, www.garethstevens.com. For a free color catalog of all our high-quality books, call toll free 1-800-542-2595 or fax 1-877-542-2596.

Library of Congress Cataloging-in-Publication Data
Names: Jacobson, Bray, author.
Title: I do karate! / Bray Jacobson.
Description: Buffalo, New York : Gareth Stevens Publishing, [2025] |
    Series: Learn to move! | Includes index.
Identifiers: LCCN 2023045839 | ISBN 9781482466010 (library binding) | ISBN
    9781482466003 (paperback) | ISBN 9781482466027 (ebook)
Subjects: LCSH: Karate–Juvenile literature. | Hand-to-hand fighting,
    Oriental–Juvenile literature.
Classification: LCC GV1114.3 .J335 2025 | DDC 796.815/3–dc23/eng/20231018
LC record available at https://lccn.loc.gov/2023045839

First Edition

Published in 2025 by
Gareth Stevens Publishing
2544 Clinton Street
Buffalo, NY 14224

Copyright © 2025 Gareth Stevens Publishing

Editor: Kristen Nelson
Designer: Leslie Taylor

Photo credits: Cover Pixel-Shot/Shutterstock.com; pp. 5, 13, 15, 24 (dojo & sensei) BearFotos/Shutterstock.com; p. 7, 24 (gi) PeopleImages.com - Yuri A/Shutterstock.com; p. 9 Geo Martinez/Shutterstock.com; p. 11 aastock/Shutterstock.com; pp. 17, 21 New Africa/Shutterstock.com; p. 19 FatCamera/iStockphoto.com; p. 23 kali9/iStockphoto.com.

Printed in the United States of America

CPSIA compliance information: Batch #CS25GS: For further information contact Gareth Stevens, New York, New York at 1-800-542-2595.

Find us on

Contents

It is time for karate class!
I go to the dojo.
This is where my class
is held.

I wear all white.
This is my uniform.
It is called a gi.

Everyone wears a belt.
The color shows our level.
Kai is a yellow belt!

We bow when class starts.
This shows respect.

My class has a teacher.
He is the sensei.

He helps us warm up.
We stretch together.

The class learns
special moves.
Lacey does a side kick.

Now we work on punches.
Ali does a forward punch.

It is the end of class.
We bow again.
Jonah thanks the sensei.
We all do!

I work hard in class.
But it is fun!

Words to Know

dojo

gi

sensei

Index